D0845982

Stay Safe!

Home Safety

Sue Barraclough

Heinemann Library
Chicago, Illinois

© 2008 Heinemann Library
a division of Reed Elsevier Inc.
Chicago, Illinois

Customer Service 888-454-2279
Visit our website at www.heinemannraintree.com

Illustrated by Paula Knight
Designed by Joanna Hinton-Malivoire
Picture research by Erica Martin
Printed and bound in China by South China Printing Co. Ltd.
12 11 10 09 08
10 9 8 7 6 5 4 3 2 1

ISBN-10-digit: 1-4034-9856-3 (hc) 1-4034-9863-6 (pb)

The Library of Congress has cataloged the first edition of this book as follows:

Barraclough, Sue.
  Home safety / Sue Barraclough.
     p. cm. -- (Stay safe.)
  Includes bibliographical references and index.
  ISBN 978-1-4034-9856-4 (hc) -- ISBN 978-1-4034-9863-2 (pb)
  1. Home accidents--Prevention--Juvenile literature. 2. Safety education--Juvenile literature. I. Title.
  TX150.B37 2008
  363.13--dc22
                                    2007016488

The paper used to print this books comes from sustainable resources.

Contents

Home is the place where you live.

Do you know how to stay safe
at home?

Never use sharp things.

Always ask a grown-up to help you cut things.

Never play with doors.

8

Always ask a grown-up to help you reach things.

Never play on the stairs.

Always stay away from hot things.

Never take pills or medicines.

Always ask a grown-up first.

Never leave things on the floor.

Always put things away.

Never touch tools or machines.

Always play far away from them.

Never touch wires and plugs.

Always ask a grown-up to switch
something on.

Always remember these safety rules.

Always stay safe at home.

Home Safety Rules

- Never play with doors.
- Never play with tools and machines.
- Ask a grown-up to help you reach things.
- Ask a grown-up to help you with sharp things.
- Ask a grown-up to help you with machines.
- Ask a grown-up before taking medicine.
- Always be careful on stairs.
- Always stay away from hot things.

Picture Glossary

machine something that helps people do a job more easily

plug something that goes into a socket to make a machine work

switch turn power on or off

Index

Note to Parents and Teachers

Books in this series teach children basic safety tips for common situations they may face. Talk about things that are dangerous at home. What things are they told not to touch? Which room do they think is the most dangerous? Tell them that more accidents happen in the kitchen than anywhere else. Ask children to study the illustrations in the book and think about whether the behavior shown is safe or dangerous. You can ask the class to think of other home safety rules and create a list for the class.

The text has been chosen with the advice of a literacy expert to ensure beginning readers success when reading independently or with moderate support.

You can support children's nonfiction literacy skills by helping students use the table of contents, picture glossary, and index.